ZODIAC BOOKS

⁕

1. A Book of Modern Verse

2. Robert Louis Stevenson
Prayers written at Vailima, & A Christmas Sermon

3. A Country Zodiac An Anthology of Prose and Verse *With woodcuts by* Thomas Bewick

4. Lewis Carroll The Hunting of the Snark
Illustrated by Mervyn Peake

5. Dr. Johnson
Some Observations and Judgements upon Life and Letters *Chosen by* John Hayward

6. Ann of Oxford Street *By* Thomas de Quincey
Illustrated by Philippe Jullian

New titles in preparation

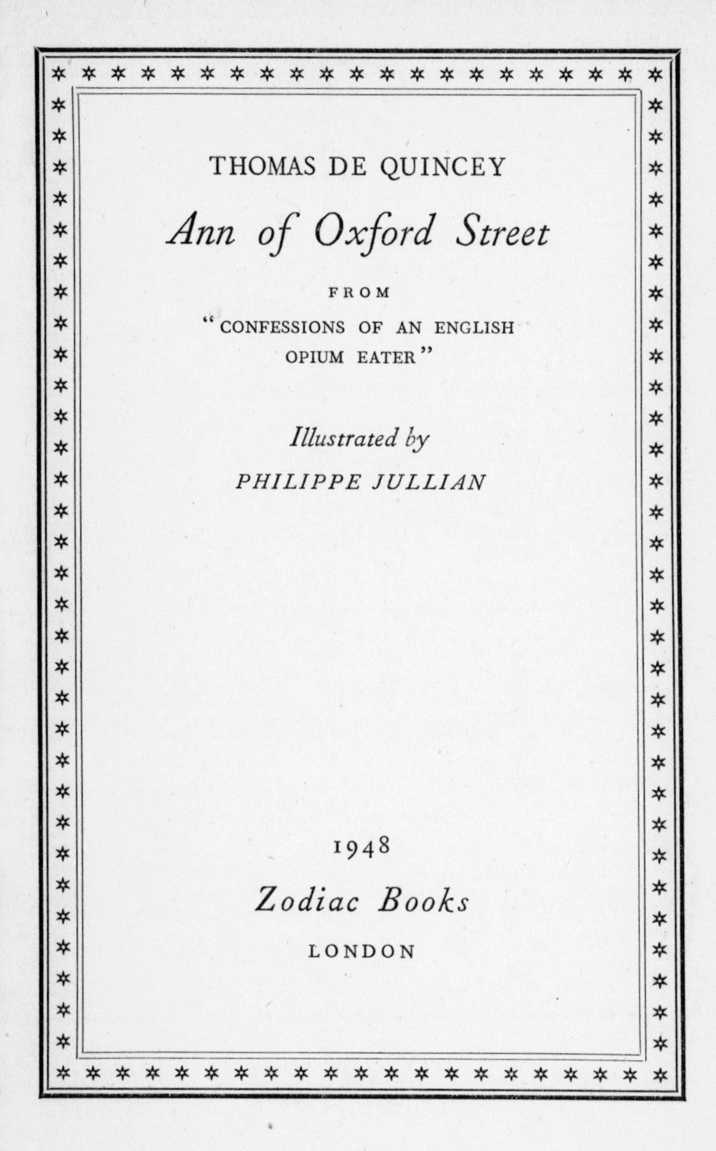

THOMAS DE QUINCEY

Ann of Oxford Street

FROM

"CONFESSIONS OF AN ENGLISH OPIUM EATER"

Illustrated by

PHILIPPE JULLIAN

1948

Zodiac Books

LONDON

Published by
LIGHTHOUSE BOOKS LTD
and distributed by
CHATTO & WINDUS
LONDON
★
CLARKE, IRWIN & CO. LTD
TORONTO

PRINTED IN GREAT BRITAIN

Ann of Oxford Street

✲

I LOST no time in opening the business which had brought me to London. By ten A.M., an hour when all men of business are presumed to be at their posts, personally or by proxy, I presented myself at the money-lender's office. My name was already known there: for I had, by letters from Wales, containing very plain and very accurate statements of my position in life and my pecuniary expectations (some of which statements it afterwards appeared that he had personally investigated and verified), endeavoured to win his favourable attention.

The money-lender, as it turned out, had one fixed rule of action. He never granted a personal interview to any man; no, not to the most beloved of his clients. One and all—myself, therefore, among the crowd—he referred for information, and for the means of prosecuting any kind of negotiation, to an attorney, who called himself, on most days of the week, by the name of Brunell, but occasionally (might it perhaps be on *red-letter* days?) by the more common name of Brown. Mr. Brunell-Brown, or Brown-Brunell, had located his hearth (if ever he had possessed one), and his household gods (when they were not in the custody of the sheriff), in Greek Street, Soho. The house was not in itself, supposing that its face had been washed now and then, at all disrespectable. But it wore an unhappy countenance of gloom and unsocial fretfulness, due in reality to the long neglect of painting, cleansing, and in some instances of repairing. There were, however, no fractured panes of glass in the windows; and the deep silence which invested the house, not only from the absence of all visitors, but also of those common household functionaries, bakers, butchers, beer-carriers, suffi-

ciently accounted for the desolation, by suggesting an excuse not strictly true—viz. that it might be tenantless. The house already had tenants through the day, though of a noiseless order, and was destined soon to increase them.

Mr. Brown-Brunell, after reconnoitring me through a narrow side-window (such as is often attached to front-doors in London), admitted me cheerfully, and conducted me, as an honoured guest, to his private *officina diplomatum* at the back of the house. From the expression of his face, but much more from the contradictory and self-counteracting play of his features, you gathered in a moment that he was a man who had much to conceal, and much, perhaps, that he would gladly forget. His eye expressed wariness against surprise, and passed in a moment into irrepressible glances of suspicion and alarm. No smile that ever his face naturally assumed but was pulled short up by some freezing counteraction, or was chased by some close-following expression of sadness. One feature there was of relenting goodness and nobleness in Mr. Brunell's character, to which it was that subsequently I myself was most profoundly indebted for an asylum that saved my life. He had the deepest, the most liberal, and unaffected love of knowledge, but, above all, of that specific knowledge which we call literature. His own stormy (and no doubt oftentimes disgraceful) career in life, that had entangled him in perpetual feuds with his fellow-men, he ascribed, with bitter imprecations, to the sudden interruption of his studies consequent upon his father's violent death, and to the necessity which threw him, at a boyish age, upon a professional life in the lower branches of law—threw him, therefore, upon daily temptations, by surrounding him with opportunities for taking advantages not strictly honourable, before he had formed any fixed principles at all. From the very first, Mr. Brunell had entered zealously into such conversations with myself as either gave openings for reviving his own delightful remembrances of classic authors, or brought up sometimes doubts for solution, sometimes perplexities and cases of intricate construction for illustration and disentanglement.

Hunger-bitten as the house and the household genius seemed, wearing the legend of *Famine* upon every mantel-piece and 'coigne of vantage,' and vehemently protesting as it must have done through all its echoes, against the introduction of supernumerary mouths, nevertheless there was (and, I suppose, of necessity) a clerk, who bore the name of Pyment, or Pyemont, then first of all, then last of all, made known to me as a possible surname. Mr. Pyment had no *alias*—or not to my knowledge—except, indeed, in the vituperative vocabulary of Mr. Brunell; in which most variegated nomenclature he bore many scores of opprobrious names, having no reference whatever to any real habits of the man, good or bad. At two rooms' distance, Mr. Brunell always assumed a minute and circumstantial knowledge of what Pyment was doing then, and what he was going to do next. All which Pyment gave himself little trouble to answer, unless it happened (as now and then it did) that he could do so with ludicrous effect. What made the necessity for Pyment was the continual call for 'an appearance' to be put in at some of the subordinate courts in Westminster—courts of conscience, sheriff courts, &c. But it happens often that he who is most indispensable, and gets through most work at one hour, becomes a useless burden at another; as the hardest working reaper seems, in the eyes of an ignoramus, on a wet, wintry day, to be a luxurious idler. Of these ups and downs in Pyment's working life Mr. Brunell made a most cynical use; making out that Pyment not only did nothing, but also that he created much work for the afflicted Brunell. However, it happened occasionally that the truth vindicated itself, by making a call upon Pyment's physics—aggressive or defensive—that needed an instant attention. 'Pyment, I say; this way, Pyment

—you're wanted, Pyment.' In fact, both were big, hulking men, and had need to be so; for sometimes, whether with good reason or none, clients at the end of a losing suit, or of a suit nominally gained, but unexpectedly laden with heavy expenses, became refractory, showed fight, and gave Pyment reason for saying that at least on this day he had earned his salary by serving an ejectment on

a client whom on any other plan it might have been hard to settle with.

But I am anticipating. I go back, therefore, for a few explanatory words, to the day of my arrival in London. How beneficial to me would a little candour have been at that early period! If (which was the simple truth, known to all parties but myself) I had been told that nothing would be brought to a close in less than six months, even assuming the ultimate adoption of my proposals, I should from the first have dismissed all hopes of this nature, as being unsuited to the practicabilities of my situation. It will be seen further on that there was a real and sincere intention of advancing the money wanted.

But it was then too late. And universally I believe myself entitled to say that even honourable lawyers will not in a case of this nature move at a faster pace: they will all alike loiter upon varied allegations through six months; and for this reason,—that any shorter period, they fancy, will hardly seem to justify, in the eyes of their client, the sum which they find themselves entitled to charge for their trouble and their preliminary correspondence. How much better for both sides, and more honourable, as more frank and free from disguises, that the client should say, 'Raise this sum' (of, suppose, £400) 'in three weeks, —which can be done, if it can be done in three years; and here is a *bonus* of £100. Delay for two months, and I decline the whole transaction.' Treated with that sort of openness, how much bodily suffering of an extreme order, and how much of the sickness from hope deferred, should I have escaped! Whereas, under the system (pursued with me as with all clients) of continually refreshing my hopes with new delusions, whiling me on with pretended preparation of deeds, and extorting from me, out of every little remittance I received from old family friends casually met in London, as much as possible for the purchase of imaginary stamps, the result was that I myself was brought to the brink of destruction through pure inanition; whilst, on the other hand, those concerned in these deceptions gained nothing that might not have been gained honourably and rightfully under a system of plain dealing.

As it was, subject to these eternal deceptions, I continued for seven or eight weeks to live most parsimoniously in lodgings. These lodgings, though barely decent in my eyes, ran away with at the least two-thirds of my remaining guineas. At length, whilst it was yet possible to reserve a solitary half-guinea towards the more urgent interest of finding daily food, I gave up my rooms, and, stating exactly the circumstances in which I stood, requested permission of Mr. Brunell to make use of his large house as a nightly asylum from the open air. Parliament had not then made it a crime, next door to a felony, for a man to sleep out-of-doors (as some twenty years later was done by our benign legislators); as yet *that* was no crime. By the law I came to know sin, and, looking back to the Cambrian hills from distant years, discovered to my surprise what a parliamentary wretch I had been in elder days, when I slept amongst cows on the open hill-sides. Lawful as yet this was; but not, therefore, less full of misery. Naturally, then, I was delighted when Mr. Brunell not only most readily assented to my request, but begged of me to come that very night, and turn the house to account as fully as I possibly could. The cheerfulness of such a concession brought with it one drawback. I now regretted that I had not, at a much earlier period, applied for this liberty; since I might thus have saved a considerable fund of guineas, applicable, of course, to all urgent necessities, but at this particular moment to one of clamorous urgency—viz. the purchase of blankets. O ancient women, daughters of toil and suffering, amongst all the hardships and bitter inheritances of flesh that ye are called upon to face, not one—not even hunger—seems in my eyes comparable to that of nightly cold. To seek a refuge from cold in bed, and then, from the thin, gauzy texture of the miserable, worn-out blankets, 'not to sleep a wink,' as Wordsworth records of poor old women in Dorsetshire, where coals, from local causes, were at the very dearest—what a terrific enemy was *that* for poor old grandmothers to face in fight! How feelingly I learned at this time, as heretofore I had learned on the wild hill-sides in Wales, what an unspeakable blessing is that of warmth! A more killing curse there does not exist for man or woman than the bitter combat between the weariness that prompts sleep and the keen, searching cold that forces you from the first access of sleep to start up horror-stricken, and to seek warmth vainly in renewed exercise, though long since fainting under fatigue. However, even without blankets, it was a fine thing to have an asylum from the open air, and to be assured of this asylum as long as I was likely to want it.

Towards nightfall I went down to Greek Street, and found, on taking possession of my new quarters, that the house already contained one single inmate,—a poor, friendless child, apparently ten years old; but she seemed hunger-bitten; and sufferings of that sort often make children look older than they are. From this forlorn child I learned that she had slept and lived there alone for some time before I came; and great joy the poor creature expressed when she found that I was in future to be her companion through the hours of darkness. The house could hardly be called large—that is, it was not large on each separate storey; but, having four storeys in all, it was large enough to impress vividly the sense of its echoing loneliness; and, from the want of furniture, the noise of the rats made a prodigious uproar on the staircase and hall; so that, amidst the real fleshly ills of cold and hunger, the forsaken child had found leisure to suffer still more from the self-created one of ghosts. Against these enemies I could promise her protection; human companionship was in itself protection; but of other and more needful aid I had, alas! little to offer. We lay upon the floor, with a bundle of law-papers for a pillow, but with no other covering than a large horseman's cloak; afterwards, however, we discovered in a garret an old sofa-cover, a small piece of rug, and some fragments of other articles, which added a little to our comfort. The poor child crept close to me for warmth, and for security against her ghostly enemies. When I was not more than usually ill, I took her into my arms, so that, in general, she was tolerably warm, and often slept when I could not; for, during the last two months of my sufferings, I slept much in the daytime, and was apt to fall into transient dozings at all hours. But my sleep distressed me more than my watching; for, besides the tumultuousness of my dreams (which were only not so awful as those which I shall have hereafter to describe as produced by opium), my sleep was never more than what is called *dog-sleep*; so that I could hear myself moaning; and very often I was awakened suddenly by my own voice. About this time, a hideous sensation began to haunt me as soon as I fell into a slumber, which has since returned upon me, at different periods of my life—viz. a sort of twitching (I knew not where, but apparently about the region of the stomach), which compelled me violently to throw out my feet for the sake of relieving it. This sensation coming on as soon as I began to sleep, and the effort to relieve it constantly awaking me, at length I slept only from exhaustion; and, through increasing weakness (as I said before), I was constantly falling asleep and constantly awaking. Too generally the very attainment of any deep repose seemed as if mechanically linked to some fatal necessity of self-interruption. It was as though a cup were gradually filled by the sleepy overflow of some natural fountain, the fulness of the cup expressing symbolically the completeness of the rest; but then, in the

next stage of the process, it seemed as though the rush and torrent-like babbling of the redundant waters, when running over from every part of the cup, interrupted the slumber which in their earlier stage of silent gathering they had so naturally produced. Such and so regular in its swell and its collapse—in its tardy growth and its violent dispersion—did this endless alternation of stealthy sleep and stormy awaking travel through stages as natural as the increments of twilight, or the kindlings of the dawn: no rest that was not a prologue to terror; no sweet tremulous pulses of restoration that did not suddenly explode through rolling clamours of fiery disruption.

Meantime, the master of the house sometimes came in upon us suddenly, and very early; sometimes not till ten o'clock; sometimes not at all. He was in constant fear of arrest. Improving on the plan of Cromwell, every night he slept in a different quarter of London; and I observed that he never failed to examine, through a private window, the appearance of those who knocked at the door, before he would allow it to be opened. He breakfasted alone; indeed, his tea equipage would hardly have admitted of his hazarding an invitation to a second person, any more than the quantity of esculent *material*, which, for the most part, was little more than a roll, or a few biscuits, purchased on his road from the place where he had slept. Or, if he *had* asked a party, as I once learnedly observed to him, the several members of it must have *stood* in the relation to each other (not *sat* in any relation whatever) of succession, and not of co-existence; in the relation of parts of time, and not of the parts of space. During his breakfast, I generally contrived a reason for lounging in; and, with an air of as much indifference as I could assume, took up such fragments as might chance to remain; sometimes, indeed, none at all remained. In doing this, I committed no robbery, except upon Mr. Brunell himself, who was thus obliged, now and then, to send out at noon for an extra biscuit; but he, through channels subsequently explained, was repaid a thousand-fold; and, as to the poor child, *she* was never admitted into his study (if I may give that name to his chief depository of parchments, law-writings, &c.); that room was to her the Bluebeard room of the house, being regularly locked on his departure to dinner, about six o'clock, which usually was his final departure for the day. Whether this child were an illegitimate daughter of Mr. Brunell, or only a servant, I could not ascertain; she did not herself know; but certainly she was treated altogether as a menial servant. No sooner did Mr. Brunell make his appearance than she went below-stairs, brushed his shoes, coat, &c.; and, except when she was summoned to run upon some errand, she never emerged from the dismal Tartarus of the kitchens to the upper air until my welcome knock towards nightfall called up her little trembling footsteps to the front-door. Of her life during the daytime, however, I knew little but what I gathered from her own account at night; for, as soon as the hours of business commenced, I saw that my absence would be acceptable; and, in general, therefore, I went off and sat in the parks or elsewhere until the approach of twilight.

But who, and what, meantime, was the master of the house himself? Reader, he was one of those anomalous practitioners in lower departments of the law who, on prudential reasons, or from necessity, deny themselves all indulgence in the luxury of too delicate a conscience. In many walks of life a conscience is a more expensive encumbrance than a wife or a carriage; and, as people talk of 'laying down' their carriages, so I suppose my friend Mr. Brunell had 'laid down' his conscience for a time; meaning, doubtless, to resume it as soon as he could afford it. He was an advertising attorney, who continually notified to the public, through the morning papers, that he undertook to raise loans for approved parties in what would generally be regarded as desperate cases—viz. where there was nothing better than *personal* security to offer. But, as he took good care to ascertain that there were ample funds in reversion to be counted on, or near connexions that would not suffer the family name to be dishonoured, and as he insured the borrower's life over a sufficient period, the risk was not great; and even of this the whole rested upon the actual money-lender, who stood aloof in the background, and never revealed himself to clients in his proper person, transacting all affairs through his proxies learned in the law,—Mr. Brunell or others. The inner economy of such a man's daily life would present a monstrous picture. Even with my limited opportunities for observing what went on, I saw scenes of intrigue and complex chicanery at which I sometimes smile to this day, and at which I smiled then in spite of my misery. My situation, however, at that time, gave me little experience, in my own person, of any qualities in Mr. Brunell's character but such as did him honour; and of his whole strange composition I ought to forget everything, but that towards me he was obliging, and, to the extent of his power, generous.

That power was not, indeed, very extensive. However, in common with the rats, I sat rent free; and, as Dr. Johnson has recorded that he never but once in his life had as much wall-fruit as he wished, so let me be grateful that, on that single occasion, I had as large a choice of rooms, or even of apartments, in a London mansion—viz., as I am now at liberty to add, at the north-west corner of Greek Street, being the house on that side the street nearest to Soho Square—as I could possibly desire. Except the Bluebeard room, which the poor child believed to be permanently haunted, and which, besides, was locked, all others, from the attics to the cellars, were at our service. 'The world was all before us,' and we pitched our tent for the night in any spot we might fancy.

This house I have described as roomy and respectable. It stands in a conspicuous situation, and in a well-known part of London. Many of my readers will have passed it, I doubt not, within a few hours of reading this. For myself, I never fail to visit it when accident draws me to London. About ten o'clock this very night (August 15, 1821, being my birthday), I turned aside from my evening walk along Oxford Street, in order to take a glance at it. It is now in the occupation of some family, apparently respectable. The windows are no longer coated by a paste composed of ancient soot and superannuated rain; and the whole exterior no longer wears an aspect of gloom. By the lights in the front drawing-room, I observed a domestic party, assembled, perhaps, at tea, and apparently cheerful and gay—marvellous contrast, in my eyes, to the darkness, cold, silence, and desolation, of that same house nineteen years ago, when its nightly occupants were one famishing scholar and a poor, neglected child. Her, by the bye, in after years, I vainly endeavoured to trace. Apart from her situation, she was not what would be called an interesting child. She was neither pretty, nor quick in understanding, nor remarkably pleasing in manners. But, thank God! even in those years I needed not the embellishments of elegant accessories to conciliate my affections. Plain human nature, in its humblest and most homely apparel, was enough for me; and I loved the child because she was my partner in wretchedness. If she is now living, she is probably a mother, with children of her own; but, as I have said, I could never trace her.

This I regret; but another person there was, at that time, whom I have since sought to trace with far deeper earnestness, and with far deeper sorrow at my failure. This person was a young woman, and one of that unhappy class who belong to the outcasts and pariahs of our female population. I feel no shame, nor have any reason to feel it, in avowing that I was then on familiar and friendly terms with many women in that unfortunate condition. Smile not, reader too carelessly facile! Frown not, reader too unseasonably austere! Little call was there here either for smiles or frowns. A penniless schoolboy could not be supposed to stand within the range of such temptations; besides that, according to the ancient Latin proverb, '*sine Cerere et Baccho*,' &c. These unhappy women, to me, were simply sisters in calamity; and sisters amongst whom, in as large measure as amongst any other equal number of persons commanding more of the world's respect, were to be found humanity, disinterested generosity, courage that would not falter in defence of the helpless, and fidelity that would have scorned to take bribes for betraying. But the truth is that at no time of my life have I been a person to hold myself polluted by the touch or approach of any creature that wore a human shape. I cannot suppose, I will not believe, that any creatures wearing the form of man or woman are so absolutely rejected and reprobate outcasts that merely to talk with them inflicts pollution. On the contrary, from my very earliest youth, it has been my

pride to converse familiarly, *more Socratico*, with all human beings—man, woman, and child—that chance might fling in my way; for a philosopher should not see with the eyes of the poor limitary creature calling himself a man of the world, filled with narrow and self-regarding prejudices of birth and education, but should look upon himself as a catholic creature, and as standing in an equal relation to high and low, to educated and uneducated, to the guilty and the innocent. Being myself, at that time, of necessity a peripatetic, or a walker of the streets, I naturally fell in more frequently with those female peripatetics who are technically called street-walkers. Some of these women had occasionally taken my part against watchmen who wished to drive me off the steps of houses where I was sitting; others had protected me against more serious aggressions. But one amongst them—the one on whose account I have at all introduced this subject—yet no! let me not class thee, O noble-minded Ann ——, with that order of women; let me find, if it be possible, some gentler name to designate the condition of her to whose bounty and compassion—ministering to my necessities when all the world stood aloof from me—I owe it that I am at this time alive. For many weeks I had walked, at nights, with this poor friendless girl up and down Oxford Street, or had rested with her on steps and under the shelter of porticos.

She could not be so old as myself: she told me, indeed, that she had not completed her sixteenth year. By such questions as my interest about her prompted, I had gradually drawn forth her simple history. Hers was a case of ordinary occurrence (as I have since had reason to think), and one in which, if London beneficence had better adapted its arrangements to meet it, the power of the law might oftener be interposed to protect and to avenge. But the stream of London charity flows in a channel which, though deep and mighty, is yet noiseless and underground;—not obvious or readily accessible to poor, houseless wanderers; and it cannot be denied that the outside air and framework of society in London, as in all vast capitals, is unavoidably harsh, cruel, and repulsive. In any case, however, I saw that part of her injuries might have been redressed; and I urged her often and earnestly to lay her complaint before a magistrate. Friendless as she was, I assured her that she would meet with immediate attention; and that English justice, which was no respecter of persons, would speedily and amply avenge her on the brutal ruffian who had plundered her little property. She promised me often that she would; but she delayed taking the steps I pointed out, from time to time; for she was timid and dejected to a degree which showed how deeply sorrow had taken hold of her young heart; and perhaps she thought justly that the most upright judge and the most righteous tribunals could do nothing to repair her heaviest wrongs. Something, however, would perhaps have been done; for it had been settled between us at length (but, unhappily, on the very last time but one that I was ever to see her) that in a day or two I, accompanied by her, should state her case to a magistrate. This little service it was destined, however, that I should never realise. Meantime, that which she rendered to me, and which was greater than I could ever have repaid her, was this:—One night, when we were pacing slowly along Oxford Street, and after a day when I had felt unusually ill and faint, I requested her to turn off with me into Soho Square. Thither we went; and we sat down on the steps of a house, which to this hour I

never pass without a pang of grief, and an inner act of homage to the spirit of that unhappy girl, in memory of the noble act which she there performed. Suddenly, as we sat, I grew much worse. I had been leaning my head against her bosom, and all at once I sank from her arms, and fell backwards on the steps. From the sensations I then had, I felt an inner conviction of the liveliest kind that, without some powerful and reviving stimulus, I should either have died on the spot, or should, at least, have sunk to a point of exhaustion from which all re-ascent, under my friendless circumstances, would soon have become hopeless. Then it was, at this crisis of my fate, that my poor orphan companion, who had herself met with little but injuries in this world, stretched out a saving hand to me. Uttering a cry of terror, but without a moment's delay, she ran off into Oxford Street, and, in less time than could be imagined, returned to me with a glass of port-wine and spices, that acted upon my empty stomach (which at that time would have rejected all solid food) with an instantaneous power of restoration; and for this glass the generous girl, without a murmur, paid out of her own humble purse, at a time, be it remembered, when she had scarcely wherewithal to purchase the bare necessaries of life, and when she could have no reason to expect that I should ever be able to reimburse her. O youthful benefactress! how often in succeeding years, standing in solitary places, and thinking of thee with grief of heart and perfect love—how often have I wished that, as in ancient times the curse of a father was believed to have a supernatural power, and to pursue its object with a fatal necessity of self-fulfilment, even so the benediction of a heart oppressed with gratitude might have a like prerogative; might have power given it from above to chase, to haunt, to waylay, to pursue thee into the central darkness of a London brothel, or (if it were possible) even into the darkness of the grave, there to awaken thee with an authentic message of peace and forgiveness, and of final reconciliation!

Some feelings, though not deeper or more passionate, are more tender than others; and often when I walk, at this time, in Oxford Street by dreary lamp-light, and hear those airs played on a common street-organ which years ago solaced me and my dear youthful companion, I shed tears, and muse with myself at the mysterious dispensation which so suddenly and so critically separated us for ever. How it happened, the reader will understand from what remains of this introductory narration.

Soon after the period of the last incident I have recorded, I met in Albemarle Street a gentleman of his late Majesty's household. This gentleman had received hospitalities, on different occasions, from my family; and he challenged me upon the strength of my family likeness. I did not attempt any disguise, but answered his questions ingenuously; and, on his pledging his word of honour that he would not betray me to my guardians, I gave him my real address in Greek Street. The next day I received from him a ten-pound banknote. The letter enclosing it was delivered, with other letters of business, to the attorney; but, though his look and manner informed me that he suspected its contents, he gave it up to me honourably, and without demur.

This present, from the particular service to which much of it was applied, leads me naturally to speak again of the original purpose which had allured me up to London, and which I had been without intermission

prosecuting through Mr. Brunell from the first day of my arrival in London.

In so mighty a world as London, it will surprise my readers that I should not have found some means of staving off the last extremities of penury; and it will strike them that two resources, at least, must have been open to me: viz. either to seek assistance from the friends of my family, or to turn my youthful accomplishments, such as they were, into some channel of pecuniary emolument. As to the first course, I may observe, generally, that what I dreaded beyond all other evils was the chance of being reclaimed by my guardians; not doubting that whatever power the law gave them would have been enforced against me to the utmost; that is, to the extremity of forcibly restoring me to the school which I had quitted,—a restoration which, as it would, in my eyes, have been a dishonour even if submitted to voluntarily, could not fail, when extorted from me in contempt and defiance of my own known wishes and earnest resistance, to have proved a humiliation worse to me than death, and which would, indeed, have terminated in death. I was, therefore, shy enough of applying for assistance even in those quarters where I was sure of receiving it, if at any risk of furnishing my guardians with a clue for tracing me. My father's friends, no doubt, had been many, and were scattered all over the kingdom; but, as to London in particular, though a large section of these friends would certainly be found there, yet (as full ten years had passed since his death) I knew very few of them even by name; and, never having seen London before—except once, in my fifteenth year, for a few hours—I knew not the address of even those few. To this mode of gaining help, therefore, in part the difficulty, but much more the danger which I have mentioned, habitually indisposed me. In regard to the other mode—that of turning any talents or knowledge that I might possess to a lucrative use—I now feel half inclined to join my reader in wondering that I should have overlooked it. As a corrector of Greek proofs (if in no other way), I might surely have gained enough for my slender wants. Such an office as this I could have discharged with an exemplary and punctual accuracy that would soon have gained me the confidence of my employers. And there was this great preliminary advantage in giving such a direction to my efforts, that the intellectual dignity and elegance associated with all ministerial services about the press would have saved my pride and self-respect from mortification. In an extreme case, such as mine had now become, I should not have absolutely disdained the humble station of 'devil.' A subaltern situation in a service inherently honourable is better than a much higher situation in a service pointing to ultimate objects that are mean or ignoble. I am, indeed, not sure that I could adequately have discharged the functions of this office. To the perfection of the diabolic character I fear that patience is one of the indispensable graces; more, perhaps, than I should be found on trial to possess for dancing attendance upon crotchety authors, superstitiously fastidious in matters of punctuation. But why talk of my qualifications? Qualified or not, where could I obtain such an office? For it must not be forgotten that even a diabolic appointment requires interest. Towards *that* I must first of all have an introduction to some respectable publisher; and this I had no means of obtaining. To say the truth, however, it had never once occurred to me to think of literary labours as a source of profit. No mode sufficiently speedy of obtaining money had ever suggested itself but that of borrowing it on the strength of my future claims and expectations. This mode I sought by every avenue to compass; and amongst other persons I applied to a Jew named D——.[1]

[1] At this period (autumn of 1856), when thirty-five years have elapsed since the first publication of these memoirs, reasons of delicacy can no longer claim respect for concealing the Jew's name, or at least the name which he adopted in his dealings with the Gentiles. I say, therefore, without scruple, that the name was Dell: and some years later it was one of the names that came before the House of Commons in connexion with something or other (I have long since forgotten *what*) growing out of the parliamentary movement against the Duke of York, in reference to Mrs. Clark, &c. Like all the other Jews with whom I have had negotiations, he was frank and honourable in his mode of conducting business. What he promised he performed; and, if his terms were high, as naturally they could not *but* be, to cover his risks, he avowed them from the first. ——To this same Mr. Dell, by the way, some eighteen months afterwards, I applied again on the same business; and, dating at that time from a respectable college, I was fortunate enough to win his serious attention to my proposals. My necessities had not arisen from any extravagance or youthful levities (these my habits forbade), but simply from the vindictive malice of my guardian, who, when he found himself no longer able to prevent me from going to the university, had, as a parting token of his regard, refused to sign an order for granting me a shilling beyond the allowance made to me at school—viz. £100 per annum. Upon this sum it was, in my time (*i.e.* in the first decennium of this century), barely possible to have lived at college; and not possible to a man who, though above the affectation of ostentatious disregard for money, and without any expensive tastes, confided, nevertheless, rather too much in servants, and did not delight in the petty details of minute economy. I soon, therefore, became embarrassed: in a movement of impatience, instead of candidly avowing my condition to my mother, or to some one of the guardians, more than one of whom would have advanced me the £250 wanted (not in his legal character of guardian, but as a private friend), I was so foolish as to engage in a voluminous negotiation with the Jew, and was put in possession of the sum I asked for, on the 'regular' terms of paying seventeen and a-half per cent by way of annuity on all the money furnished; Israel, on his part, graciously resuming no more than about ninety guineas of the said money, on account of an attorney's bill (for what services, to whom rendered, and when—whether at the siege of Jerusalem, or at the building of the Second Temple—I have not yet discovered). How many perches this bill measured I really forget; but I still keep it in a cabinet of natural curiosities.

To this Jew, and to other advertising money-lenders, I had introduced myself, with an account of my expectations; which account they had little difficulty in ascertaining to be correct. The person there mentioned as the second son of —— was found to have all the claims (or more than all) that I had stated: but one question still remained, which the faces of the Jews pretty significantly suggested,—was I that person? This doubt had never occurred to me as a possible one; I had rather feared, whenever my Jewish friends scrutinised me keenly, that I might be too well known to be that person, and that some scheme might be passing in their minds for entrapping me and selling me to my guardians. It was strange to me to find my own self, *materialiter* considered (so I expressed it, for I doated on logical accuracy of distinctions), suspected of counterfeiting my own self, *formaliter* considered. However, to satisfy their scruples, I took the only course in my power. Whilst I was in Wales, I had received various letters from young friends; these I produced, for I carried them constantly in my pocket. Most of these letters were from the Earl of Altamont, who was at that time, and had been for some years back, amongst my confidential friends. These were dated from Eton. I had also some from the Marquis of Sligo, his father; who, though absorbed in agricultural pursuits, yet having been an Etonian himself, and as good a scholar as a nobleman needs to be, still retained an affection for classical studies and for youthful scholars. He had, accordingly, from the time that I was fifteen, corresponded with me—sometimes upon the great improvements which he had made, or was meditating, in the counties of Mayo and Sligo, since I had been there; sometimes upon the merits of a Latin poet; at other times, suggesting subjects on which he fancied that I could write verses myself, or breathe poetic inspiration into the mind of my once familiar companion, his son.

On reading the letters, one of my Jewish friends agreed to furnish two or three hundred pounds on my personal security, provided I could persuade the young earl—who was, by the way, not older than myself—to

guarantee the payment on our joint coming of age; the Jew's final object being, as I now suppose, not the trifling profit he could expect to make by me, but the prospect of establishing a connexion with my noble friend, whose great expectations were well known to him. In pursuance of this proposal on the part of the Jew, about eight or nine days after I had received the £10, I prepared to visit Eton. Nearly three guineas of the money I had given to my money-lending friend in the background; or, more accurately, I had given that sum to Mr. Brunell, *alias* Brown, as representing Mr. Dell, the Jew; and a smaller sum I had given directly to himself, on his own separate account. What he alleged in excuse for thus draining my purse at so critical a moment was that stamps must be bought, in order that the writings might be prepared whilst I was away from London. I thought in my heart that he was lying, but I did not wish to give him any excuse for charging his own delays upon me. About fifteen shillings I had employed in re-establishing (though in a very humble way) my dress. Of the remainder, I gave one-quarter (something more than a guinea) to Ann, meaning, on my return, to have divided with her whatever might remain.

These arrangements made, soon after six o'clock, on a dark winter evening, I set off, accompanied by Ann, towards Piccadilly; for it was my intention to go down as far as the turn to Salt Hill and Slough on the Bath or Bristol mail. Our course lay through a part of the town which has now totally disappeared, so that I can no longer retrace its ancient boundaries—having been replaced by Regent Street and its adjacencies. *Swallow Street* is all that I remember of the names superseded by this large revolutionary usurpation. Having time enough before us, however, we bore away to the left, until we came into Golden Square. There, near the corner of Sherrard Street, we sat down, not wishing to part in the tumult and blaze of Piccadilly. I had told Ann of my plans some time before, and now I assured her again that she should share in my good fortune, if I met with any, and that I would never forsake her, as soon as I had power to protect her. This I fully intended, as much from inclination as from a sense of duty; for, setting aside gratitude (which in any case must have made me her debtor for life), I loved her as affectionately as if she had been my sister; and at this moment with sevenfold tenderness, from pity at witnessing her extreme dejection. I had apparently most reason for dejection, because I was leaving the saviour of my life; yet I, considering the shock my health had received, was cheerful and full of hope. She, on the contrary, who was parting with one who had had little means of serving her, except by kindness and brotherly treatment, was overcome by sorrow, so that when I kissed her at our final farewell, she put her arms about my neck, and wept, without speaking a word. I hoped to return in a week, at furthest, and I agreed with her that, on the fifth night from that, and every night afterwards, she should wait for me, at six o'clock near the bottom of Great Titchfield Street; which had formerly been our customary haven of rendezvous, to prevent our missing each other in the great Mediterranean of Oxford Street. This, and other measures of precaution, I took; one, only, I forgot. She had either never told me, or (as a matter of no great interest) I had forgotten, her surname. It is a general practice, indeed, with girls of humble rank in her unhappy condition, not (as novel-reading women of higher pretensions) to style themselves *Miss Douglas*, *Miss Montague*, &c., but simply by their Christian names, *Mary*, *Jane*, *Frances*, &c. Her surname, as the surest means of tracing her, I ought now to have inquired; but the truth is, having no reason to think that our meeting again could, in consequence of a short interruption, be more difficult or uncertain than it had been for so many weeks, I scarcely for a moment adverted to it as necessary, or placed it amongst my memoranda against this parting interview; and, my final anxieties being spent in comforting her with hopes, and in pressing upon her the necessity of getting some medicine for a violent cough with which she was troubled,

I wholly forgot this precaution until it was too late to recall her.

When I reached the Gloucester Coffee-house in Piccadilly, at which, in those days, all the western mails stopped for a few minutes in going out of London, it was already a quarter-of-an-hour past eight o'clock; the Bristol Mail was on the point of going off, and I mounted on the outside. The fine fluent motion [1] of this mail soon laid me asleep. It is somewhat remarkable that the first easy or refreshing sleep which I had enjoyed for some months was on the outside of a mail-coach—a bed which, at this day, I find rather an uneasy one. Connected with this sleep was a little incident which served, as hundreds of others did at that time, to convince me how easily a man who has never been in any great distress may pass through life without knowing in his own person, and experimentally testing, the possible goodness of the human heart, or, as unwillingly I add, its possible churlishness. So thick a curtain of *manners* is drawn over the features and expression of men's natures that, to the ordinary observer, the two extremities, and the infinite field of varieties which lie between them, are all confounded under one neutral disguise. The case was this:—For the first four or five miles out of London, I annoyed my fellow-passenger on the roof by occasionally falling against him when the coach gave a lurch; and, indeed, if the road had been less smooth and level than it was, I should have fallen off from weakness. Of this annoyance he complained heavily; as, perhaps, in the

[1] The Bristol Mail was at that time the best appointed in the kingdom—owing that advantage, first of all, to an unusually good road—and this advantage it shared with the Bath Mail (their route being exactly the same for a hundred and five miles); but, secondly, it had the separate advantage of an *extra* sum for expenses subscribed by the Bristol merchants.

same circumstances, most people would. He expressed his complaint, however, more morosely than the occasion seemed to warrant; and, if I had parted with him at that moment, I should have thought of him as a surly and almost brutal fellow. Still I was conscious that I had given him some cause for complaint; and therefore I apologised, assuring him that I would do what I could to avoid falling asleep for the future; and, at the same time, in as few words as possible, I explained to him that I was ill, and in a weak state from long suffering, and that I could not afford to take an inside place. The man's manner changed upon hearing this explanation in an instant: and, when I next woke for a minute, from the noise and lights of Hounslow (for, in spite of my efforts, I had again fallen asleep within two minutes), I found that he had put his arm round me to protect me from falling off; and for the rest of my journey he behaved to me with the gentleness of a woman. And this was the more kind, as he could not have known that I was not going the whole way to Bath or Bristol. Unfortunately, indeed, I *did* go further than I intended; for so genial and refreshing was my sleep, being in the open air, that, upon the sudden pulling up of the mail (possibly at a post-office), I found that we had reached some place six or seven miles to the west of Salt Hill. Here I alighted; and, during the half-minute that the mail stopped, I was entreated by my friendly companion (who, from the transient glimpse I had of him under the glaring lights of Piccadilly, might be a respectable upper servant) to go to bed without delay. This, under the feeling that some consideration was due to one who had done me so seasonable a service, I promised, though with no intention of doing so; and, in fact, I immediately moved forward on foot.

It must then have been nearly eleven; but so slowly did I creep along that I heard a clock in a cottage strike four as I was on the point of turning down the road from Slough to Eton. The air and the sleep had both refreshed me; but I was weary, nevertheless. I remember a thought (obvious enough, and pointedly expressed by a Roman

poet) which gave me some consolation, at that moment, under my poverty. There had been, some weeks before, a murder committed on Hounslow Heath, which at that time was really a heath, entirely unenclosed, and exhibiting a sea-like expanse in all directions, except one. I cannot be mistaken when I say that the name of the murdered person was *Steele*, and that he was the owner of a lavender plantation in that neighbourhood.[1] Every

[1] Two men, Holloway and Haggerty, were long afterwards convicted, upon very questionable evidence, as the perpetrators of this murder. The main testimony against them was that of a Newgate turnkey, who had imperfectly overheard a conversation between the two men. The current impression was that of great dissatisfaction with the evidence; and this impression was strengthened by the pamphlet of an acute lawyer,

step of my regress (for I now walked with my face towards London) was bringing me nearer to the heath; and it naturally occurred to me that I and the accursed murderer, if he were that night abroad, might, at every instant, be unconsciously approaching each other through the darkness; in which case, said I, supposing myself—instead of being little better than an outcast,

'*Lord of my learning, and no land beside*'—

like my friend Lord Altamont, heir, by general repute, to £30,000 per annum, what a panic should I be under at this moment about my throat! Indeed, it was not likely that Lord Altamont should ever be in my situation; but, nevertheless, the spirit of the remark remains true, that vast power and possessions make a man shamefully afraid of dying; and I am convinced that many of the most intrepid adventurers who, being poor, enjoy the full use of their natural energies, would, if at the very instant of going into action news were brought to them that they had unexpectedly succeeded to an estate in England of £50,000 a-year, feel their dislike to bullets furiously sharpened,[1] and their efforts at self-possession proportionately difficult. So true it is, in the language

exposing the unsoundness and incoherency of the statements relied upon by the court. They were executed, however, in the teeth of all opposition. And, as it happened that an enormous wreck of life occurred at the execution (not fewer, I believe, than sixty persons having been trampled under foot by the unusual pressure of some brewers' draymen forcing their way with linked arms to the space below the drop), this tragedy was regarded for many years by a section of the London mob as a providential judgment upon the passive metropolis.

[1] It will be objected that many men, of the highest rank and wealth, have, notwithstanding, in our own day, as well as throughout our history, been amongst the foremost in courting danger on the field of battle. True; but this is not the case supposed. Long familiarity with power and with wealth has, to them, deadened their effect and attractions.

of a wise man, whose own experience had made him acquainted equally with good and evil fortune, that riches are better fitted

> '*To slacken virtue, and abate her edge,*
> *Than tempt her to do aught may merit praise.*'
>
> PARADISE REGAINED

I dally with my subject, because, to myself, the remembrance of these times is profoundly interesting. But my reader shall not have any further cause to complain; for now I hasten to its close. In the road between Slough and Eton I fell asleep; and, just as the morning began to dawn, I was awakened by the voice of a man standing over me, and apparently studying my *physics*, whilst to me—upon so sudden an introduction to him in so suspicious a situation—his *morals* naturally suggested a more interesting subject of inquiry. I know not what he was. He was an ill-looking fellow, but not, therefore, of necessity, an ill-meaning fellow; or, if he were, I suppose he thought that no person sleeping out-of-doors in winter could be worth robbing. In which conclusion, however, as it regarded myself, I have the honour to assure him, supposing him ever to find himself amongst my readers, that he was entirely mistaken. I was not sorry at his disturbance, as it roused me to pass through Eton before people were generally astir. The night had been heavy and misty; but towards the morning it had changed to a slight frost, and the trees were now covered with rime.

I slipped through Eton unobserved; washed myself, and as far as possible adjusted my dress, at a little public-house in Windsor; and, about eight o'clock, went down towards the precincts of the college, near which were congregated the houses of the 'Dames.' On my road I met some junior boys, of whom I made inquiries. An Etonian is always a gentleman; and, in spite of my shabby habiliments, they answered me civilly. My friend Lord Altamont was gone to Jesus College, Cambridge. 'Ibi omnis effusus labor!' I had, however, other friends at Eton; but it is not to all who wear that name in prosperity that a man is willing to present himself in distress. On recollecting myself, however, I asked for the Earl of Desart,[1] to whom (though my acquaintance with him was not so intimate as with some others) I should not have shrunk from presenting myself under any circumstances. He was still at Eton, though, I believe, on the wing for Cambridge. I called, was received kindly, and asked to breakfast.

Lord Desart placed before me a magnificent breakfast. It was really such; but in my eyes it seemed trebly magnificent from being the first regular meal, the first 'good man's table,' that I had sat down to for months. Strange to say, I could scarcely eat anything. On the day when I first received my ten-pound bank-note, I had gone to a baker's shop and bought a couple of rolls; this very shop I had some weeks before surveyed with an eagerness of desire which it was humiliating to recollect. I remembered the story (which, however, I now believed to be a falsehood) about Otway, and feared that there might be danger in eating too rapidly. But there was no cause for alarm; my appetite was utterly gone, and I nauseated food

[1] I had known Lord Desart, the eldest son of a very large family, some years earlier, when bearing the title of Lord Castlecuffe. Cuffe was the family name; and I believe that they traced their descent from a person of some historic interest—viz. that Cuffe who was secretary to the unhappy Earl of Essex during his treasonable *émeute* against the government of Queen Elizabeth.

of every kind. This effect, from eating what approached to a meal, I continued to feel for weeks. On the present occasion, at Lord Desart's table, I found myself not at all better than usual; and, in the midst of luxuries, appetite I had none. I had, however, unfortunately, at all times a craving for wine: I explained my situation, therefore, to Lord Desart, and gave him a short account of my late sufferings; with which he expressed deep sympathy, and called for wine. This gave me instantaneous relief and immoderate pleasure; and on all occasions, when I had an opportunity, I never failed to drink wine. Obvious it is, however, that this indulgence in wine would continue to strengthen my malady, for the tone of my stomach was apparently quite sunk; but, by a better regimen, it might sooner, and, perhaps, effectually, have been restored.

I hope that it was not from this love of wine that I lingered in the neighbourhood of my Eton friends; I persuaded myself *then* that it was from reluctance to ask Lord Desart, on whom I was conscious of having no sufficient claims, the particular service in quest of which I had come to Eton. I was, however, unwilling to lose my journey, and—I asked it. Lord Desart, whose good-nature was unbounded, and which, in regard to myself, had been measured rather by his compassion, perhaps, for my condition, and his knowledge of my intimacy with several of his relatives, than by an over-rigorous inquiry into the extent of my own direct claims, faltered, nevertheless, at this request. He acknowledged that he did not like to have any dealings with money-lenders, and feared lest such a transaction might come to the ears of his connexions. Moreover, he doubted whether *his* signature, whose expectations were so much more bounded than those of his cousin, would avail with my unchristian friends. Still he did not wish, apparently, to mortify me by a refusal peremptory and absolute; for, after a little consideration, he promised, under certain conditions, which he pointed out, to give his security. Lord Desart was at this time not above eighteen years of age; but I have often doubted, on recollecting since the good sense and prudence which on this occasion he mingled with so much urbanity of manner (which in him wore the grace of youthful sincerity), whether any statesman, the oldest and the most accomplished in diplomacy, could have acquitted himself better under the same circumstances.

Re-comforted by this promise, which was not quite equal to the best, but far above the worst that I had anticipated, I returned in a Windsor coach to London three days after I had quitted it. And now I come to the end of my story. The Jews did not approve of Lord Desart's conditions, or so they said. Whether they would in the end have acceded to them, and were only seeking time for making further inquiries, I know not; but many delays were made—time passed on—the small fragment of my bank-note had just melted away, and before any conclusion could have been put to the business I must have relapsed into my former state of wretchedness. Suddenly, at this crisis, an opening was made, almost by accident, for reconciliation with my guardians. I quitted London in haste, and returned to the Priory; after some time, I proceeded to Oxford; and it was not until many months had passed away that I had it in my power again to revisit the ground which had become so interesting to me, and to this day remains so, as the chief scene of my youthful sufferings.

Meantime, what had become of Ann? Where was she? Whither had she gone? According to our agreement, I

sought her daily, and waited for her every night, so long as I staid in London, at the corner of Titchfield Street; and during the last days of my stay in London I put into activity every means of tracing her that my knowledge of London suggested, and the limited extent of my power made possible. The street where she had lodged I knew, but not the house; and I remembered, at last, some account which she had given of ill-treatment from her landlord, which made it probable that she had quitted those lodgings before we parted. She had few acquaintance; most people, besides, thought that the earnestness of my inquiries arose from motives which moved their laughter or their slight regard; and others, thinking that I was in chase of a girl who had robbed me of some trifles, were naturally and excusably indisposed to give me any clue to her, if indeed they had any to give. Finally, as my despairing resource, on the day I left London I put into the hands of the only person who (I was sure) must know Ann by sight, from having been in company with us once or twice, an address to the Priory. All was in vain. To this hour I have never heard a syllable about her. This, amongst such troubles as most men meet with in this life, has been my heaviest affliction. If she lived, doubtless we must have been sometimes in search of each other, at the very same moment, through the mighty labyrinths of London; perhaps even within a few feet of each other—a barrier no wider, in a London street, often amounting in the end to a separation for eternity! During some years I hoped that she *did* live; and I suppose that, in the literal and unrhetorical use of the word *myriad*, I must, on my different visits to London, have looked into many myriads of female faces, in the hope of meeting Ann. I should know her again amongst a thousand, and if seen

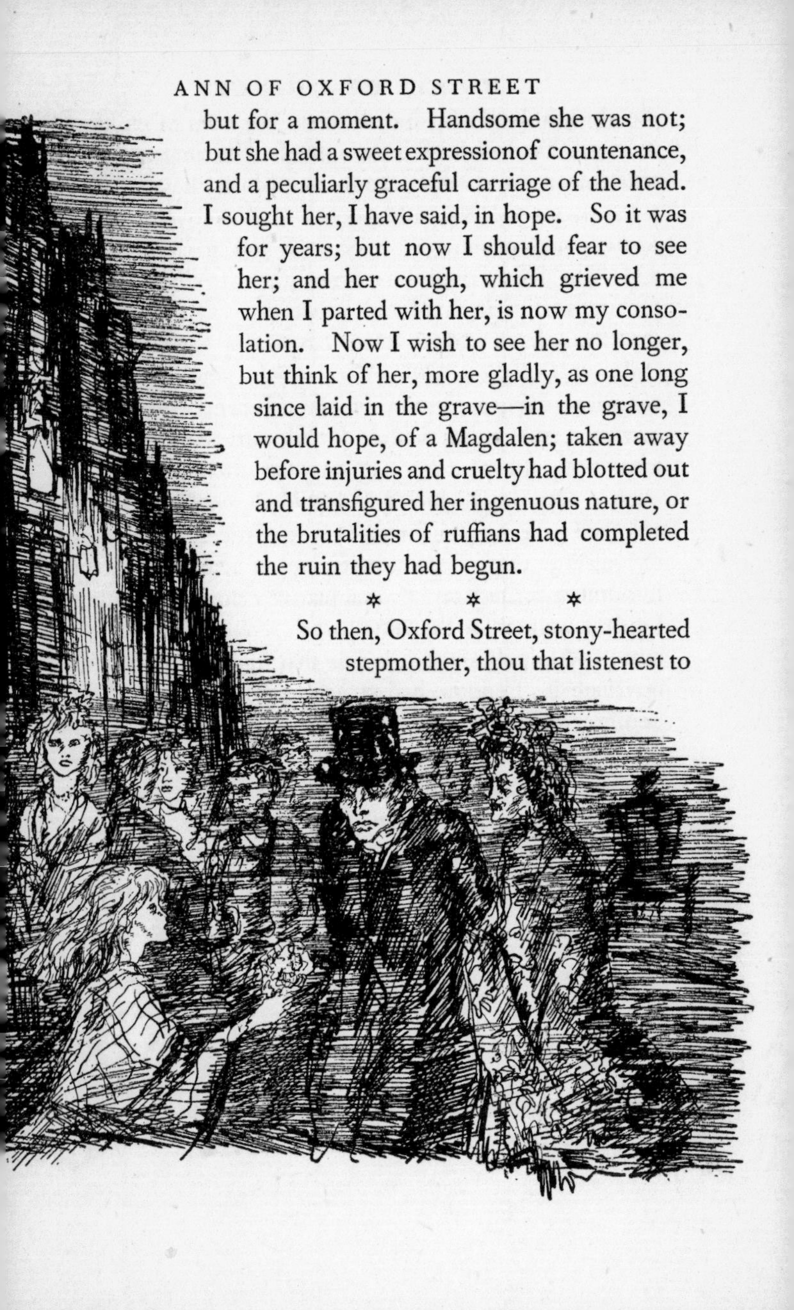

but for a moment. Handsome she was not; but she had a sweet expression of countenance, and a peculiarly graceful carriage of the head. I sought her, I have said, in hope. So it was for years; but now I should fear to see her; and her cough, which grieved me when I parted with her, is now my consolation. Now I wish to see her no longer, but think of her, more gladly, as one long since laid in the grave—in the grave, I would hope, of a Magdalen; taken away before injuries and cruelty had blotted out and transfigured her ingenuous nature, or the brutalities of ruffians had completed the ruin they had begun.

* * *

So then, Oxford Street, stony-hearted stepmother, thou that listenest to the sighs of orphans, and drinkest the tears of children, at length I was dismissed from thee! The time was come that I no more should pace in anguish thy never-ending terraces, no more should wake and dream in captivity to the pangs of hunger. Successors too many to myself and Ann have, doubtless, since then trodden in our footsteps, inheritors of our calamities. Other orphans than Ann have sighed; tears have been shed by other children; and thou, Oxford Street, hast since those days echoed to the groans of innumerable hearts. For myself, however, the storm which I had outlived seemed to have been the pledge of a long fair weather; the premature sufferings which I had paid down to have been accepted as a ransom for many years to come, as a price of long immunity from sorrow; and, if again I walked in London, a solitary and contemplative man (as oftentimes I did), I walked for the most part in serenity and peace of mind. And, although it is true that the calamities of my novitiate in London had struck root so deeply in my bodily constitution that afterwards they shot up and flourished afresh, and grew into a noxious umbrage that has overshadowed and darkened my latter years, yet these second assaults of suffering were met with a fortitude more confirmed, with the resources of a maturer intellect, and with alleviations, how deep! from sympathising affection.

PRINTED BY
R. AND R. CLARK, LTD., EDINBURGH